CONSPIRACY THEORIES THAT WERE TRUE

ETHAN HAYES

FREE REIGN

Copyright © 2023 by Ethan Hayes
Published by Free Reign Publishing

This book or any portion thereof may not be reproduced or used in any manner whatsoever without the express written permission of the publisher except for the use of brief quotations in a book review. All rights reserved.

ISBN 13: 978-1-953462-97-8

Free Reign Publishing, LLC
San Diego, CA

Contents

Introduction	v
Chapter 1 *OPERATION MOCKINGBIRD*	1
Chapter 2 *TUSKEGEE SYPHILIS EXPERIMENT*	11
Chapter 3 *MK-ULTRA*	21
Chapter 4 *COINTELPRO*	33
Chapter 5 *OPERATION NORTHWOODS*	41
PUBLISHER'S EXCERPT	47
PUBLISHER'S EXCERPT 2	59
Chapter 6 *THE HEART ATTACK GUN*	65
Chapter 7 *OPERATION SNOW WHITE*	71
Chapter 8 *OPERATION PAPERCLIP*	81
Chapter 9 *THE US PUBLIC HEALTH SERVICE SYPHILIS STUDY IN GUATEMALA*	91
Chapter 10 *OPERATION LAC (LARGE AREA COVERED)*	101
CONCLUSION	109
About the Author	113
Also by Ethan Hayes	115
Also by Free Reign Publishing	117

Introduction

In the dark corners of whispered conversations and the labyrinthine pathways of the internet, conspiracy theories have long found fertile ground to take root. To many, these tales are but the outlandish products of overactive imaginations, often dismissed with a wave of the hand or a skeptical eye roll. Yet, while the world is awash with unfounded speculation, every so often, a conspiracy theory emerges from the shadows to reveal itself as undeniable fact. *Conspiracy Theories That Were True* delves deep into these once-mocked narratives, shining a light on the stories that were met with incredulity only to later be proven true.

In this exploration, we journey through time, unearthing episodes that have both shocked and altered the course of history. From government cover-ups and corporate scandals to secret societies and hidden agendas, this book is an invitation to reimagine what we think we know. It's a testament to the age-old adage that, sometimes, truth is stranger than fiction.

Prepare to have your perceptions challenged and beliefs shaken, as we uncover the real stories behind some of the most infamous conspiracies that turned out to be true.

Ethan Hayes

Chapter 1
OPERATION MOCKINGBIRD

OPERATION MOCKINGBIRD WAS a covert project undertaken by the U.S. Central Intelligence Agency (CIA) to influence media and the coverage of events, both domestic and international. While the details and scale of the operation have been a matter of debate, some aspects of the program are documented.

ORIGINS:

After World War II ended in 1945, the geopolitical landscape was marked by increasing tension between the United States and the Soviet Union, two superpowers with contrasting ideologies — democracy and capitalism versus communism. This tension eventually blossomed into the Cold War.

Both the U.S. and the USSR recognized the power of propaganda early on. As they vied for global influence, both superpowers sought to spread their respective narratives and ideologies. This battle of narratives was as integral to the Cold War as the arms race or any physical skirmish.

In order to battle on the propaganda front, the U.S. needed expand its intelligence operations. The OSS (Office of Strategic Services) had been shut down in 1945 with the end of World War 2; but just opening it back up wasn't enough. If the U.S. was going to compete against the Soviet Union, it needed a new agency with vast powers and that would be the CIA.

The CIA was established in 1947 through the National Security Act. One of its primary objectives was gathering intelligence from abroad, but its role soon expanded to covert operations to counter communist influence worldwide and one way to do that was through propaganda.

In 1948, the Office of Policy Coordination was established within the CIA. The OPC was the covert action branch responsible for psychological warfare and other forms of non-overt military action. Frank Wisner, a seasoned intelligence operative, was appointed to head the OPC.

Frank Wisner was a staunch anti-communist. He believed fervently in the power of propaganda and recognized the need for the U.S. to engage in its own propaganda efforts to counteract Soviet influence. Under his direction, the OPC sought to harness and direct the power of the media.

GENESIS OF OPERATION MOCKINGBIRD:

Wisner often referred to his propaganda campaign as his "Mighty Wurlitzer," an organ capable of playing any propaganda tune he desired. The idea was to have a network of journalists and media outlets that could be used to disseminate and amplify CIA-approved narratives.

Wisner tapped into his network of contacts in the media and began recruiting journalists. Some sources suggest that journalists from every major news outlet, including CBS, The New York Times, and The Washington Post, were involved in some capacity. Some were on the payroll, while others cooperated based on shared ideologies or personal relationships.

Beyond just spreading propaganda, these journalists

also acted as information channels, providing the CIA with valuable intel from their sources.

The operation wasn't limited to domestic media. The CIA sought to establish a media presence in foreign countries as well. This sometimes involved funding or supporting foreign publications that would be sympathetic to U.S. interests.

EXPANSION AND INSTITUTIONALIZATION:

As the operation grew, the CIA established more formalized ties with journalists, media outlets, and student/cultural organizations. The media's influence was recognized as a potent tool not just for counteracting enemy propaganda but also for shaping the narrative in regions of interest to the U.S., such as Latin America, the Middle East, and Southeast Asia.

While "Mockingbird" is the name most commonly associated with this operation in popular culture, official documents and investigations, like the Church Committee's reports, do not always use this term. It is unclear whether "Mockingbird" was an official codename or an informal designation. The precise starting point of the operation, like many covert operations, is somewhat muddled. Still, its roots can clearly be traced back to the early days of the Cold War and the CIA's establishment.

It's essential to note that the lines between information gathering, influence campaigns, and mere association with intelligence agencies can be blurry. Not every journalist or media outlet allegedly connected with the CIA was necessarily involved in a nefarious capacity. Some might have provided occasional information, some might have been unwitting participants, and others might have collaborated more directly.

The purported influence went beyond news media. It's believed the CIA sought to sway the arts, funding writers, magazines, and cultural programs that aligned with their views.

CONSPIRACY THEORY BECOMES FACT:

Staunch opponents of the CIA often cited theories the agency was peddling propaganda through the airwaves and in print within the United States. However, those voices were often marginalized and mocked as *conspiracy theorists* by the same media the CIA had put on the payroll, but mistrust of government was growing.

In 1974, Seymour Hersh, an investigative journalist with The New York Times, published a ground-breaking article revealing illegal activities by the CIA, including spying on American citizens. His revelations suggested that the CIA had overstepped its mandate (the CIA is supposed to operate only outside of the U.S. and is prohibited from domestic spying).

In response to the mounting concerns and the exposé by Hersh, the U.S. Senate established a select committee in January 1975 to investigate and review the intelligence activities of agencies like the CIA, FBI, and NSA.

The committee was officially called the "U.S. Senate Select Committee to Study Governmental Operations with Respect to Intelligence Activities," but it became popularly known as the "Church Committee" after its chairman, Senator Frank Church of Idaho.

While the immediate trigger for the committee's creation was the revelation of domestic spying, its mandate was broad. It aimed to investigate intelligence abuses across the board, spanning multiple administrations, both Democratic and Republican.

As part of its broad mandate, the Church Committee delved into the CIA's relationships with the media. It unearthed a program where the CIA sought to influence domestic and international media, a program that has since been popularly (though not officially) referred to as Operation Mockingbird.

Committee Findings:
- The committee found that the CIA maintained a network of individuals in the U.S. media to help disseminate and amplify its messages.
- The CIA had paid relationships with reporters from major media outlets, including but not limited to The New York Times, The Washington Post, and CBS.
- These relationships were, at times, deeper than merely relaying information. The CIA occasionally funded news articles and even books that advanced its interests.
- Internationally, the CIA attempted to (and sometimes successfully did) plant propaganda in foreign news outlets.

As these findings were publicized, the reaction from the implicated media houses was mixed. Some denied knowledge, while others defended their cooperation in the context of national security during the Cold War.

Post the Church Committee's investigations and revelations, the CIA formally announced its intention to cease paid relationships with journalists and media institutions. Whether and to what extent the CIA adhered to this policy remains a matter of debate.

The Church Committee's investigations culminated in 14 published reports in 1975-1976, detailing a wide array of intelligence abuses. As a direct result of its work, significant reforms were initiated:

- **Foreign Intelligence Surveillance Act (FISA)**: Enacted in 1978, FISA set up a separate legal regime for foreign intelligence surveillance carried out in the U.S., including the establishment of the FISA Court to oversee surveillance warrants.
- **Senate Select Committee on Intelligence**: The Church Committee recommended the creation of permanent Senate and House committees to oversee intelligence activities. The Senate Select Committee on Intelligence was thus established in 1976, followed by a similar committee in the House.

While the Church Committee wasn't formed specifically because of Operation Mockingbird, its broad mandate and the climate of distrust towards governmental agencies in the mid-1970s led it to unearth and reveal the CIA's covert media relationships, providing a more transparent view of the depths of the intelligence community's domestic operations.

21ST CENTURY VERSION OF OPERATION MOCKINGBIRD?":

A U.S. federal judge has prohibited officials from President Joe Biden's administration from reaching out to social media platforms regarding content control.

Judge Terry Doughty granted the injunction on Tuesday, following a legal challenge initiated by the Republican attorneys general of Louisiana and Missouri. They claim that the government overstepped its boundaries by urging social media companies to combat misinformation.

Doughty wrote that the government's attempt to limit false claims related to elections and the COVID-19 pandemic *"arguably involves the most massive attack against free speech in United States history"*.

This ban comes on the heels of Elon Musk, owner of Twitter / X, accusing the State Department's Global Engagement Center (GEC) of *'censorship and media manipulation'*. Journalist, Matt Taibbi described the GEC as a "fledgling analytic/intelligence" arm to participate in guiding Twitter's moderation of content and how it often used the media to clash with the tech giant beginning in February 2020 as the coronavirus pandemic was underway. Taibbi continued:

> "The GEC flagged accounts as 'Russian personas and proxies' based on criteria like, 'Describing the Coronavirus as an engineered bioweapon,' blaming 'research conducted at the Wuhan institute,' and 'attributing the appearance of the virus to the CIA,'" Taibbi wrote. "State also flagged accounts that retweeted news that Twitter banned the popular U.S. ZeroHedge, claiming the episode 'led to another flurry of disinformation narratives.' ZH had done reports speculating that the virus had lab origin."

Is Operation Mockingbird still underway? Has it spread from the CIA to other government intelligence and law enforcement agencies? Skeptics of government say it has, but like before, the media describes those claims as mere…conspiracy theories.

Chapter 2
TUSKEGEE SYPHILIS EXPERIMENT

THE TUSKEGEE SYPHILIS EXPERIMENT, also known as the Tuskegee Study of Untreated Syphilis in the Negro Male, is one of the most infamous cases of unethical human experimentation in U.S. history, and at one time was considered a conspiracy theory. The study was initially supposed to last six months but ended up continuing for 40 years, from 1932 to 1972.

ORIGINS:

The study began in 1932 in Macon County, Alabama, and was conducted by the U.S. Public Health Service (USPHS).

Dr. Taliaferro Clark was the original architect of

the study. Initially, Dr. Clark intended the study to be a short-term project to record the progression of syphilis and then offer treatment. However, under subsequent leadership, the study's purpose shifted to observing the long-term effects of untreated syphilis.

KEY FIGURES / **INSTITUTIONS OVER THE YEARS:**

The initiation and continuation of the Tuskegee Syphilis Experiment were facilitated by a combination of institutional decisions by the USPHS, complicit actions by key individuals, and the broader societal context of racial discrimination and unequal access to healthcare. The study's prolonged duration, despite clear ethical violations, is a testament to the systemic issues that allowed such an experiment to persist for four decades.

- **Dr. Raymond Vonderlehr**: He succeeded Dr. Clark and became the on-site director of the study. Under his leadership, the intention of the study was redefined to observe untreated syphilis in black males until their deaths. Vonderlehr developed the procedures for the study and

was involved in its operations for many years.
- **Dr. John Heller**: He was another central figure in the study who directed it for a significant portion of its duration, particularly during the years after World War II. Under his tenure, the withholding of treatment continued, even after penicillin was recognized as a standard and effective treatment for syphilis.
- **Dr. Oliver Wenger**: While not directly overseeing the study, Wenger was a key figure in the USPHS's venereal disease section and supported the Tuskegee experiment.
- **Tuskegee Institute**: The Tuskegee Institute (now Tuskegee University), a historically black college in Alabama, played a role in the study. The USPHS collaborated with the Institute, which provided logistical support and helped gain the trust of the local community. However, it's essential to note that the primary responsibility and decision-making authority for the study's design and continuation lay with the USPHS.

- **Dr. Eugene Dibble**: He was the head of the John Andrew Hospital at the Tuskegee Institute and was involved in the study, mainly in its early stages.
- **Eunice Rivers**: She was a black nurse who played a significant role in the day-to-day operations of the study. Rivers was responsible for maintaining contact with the participants, ensuring they attended scheduled appointments, and acted as a bridge between the researchers and the community. Because of her involvement and trust within the community, many participants stayed in the study.

MAIN FEATURES OF THE EXPERIMENT:

The study involved 600 black men, of which 399 had syphilis and 201 did not. The men were told they were being treated for "bad blood," a colloquial term used in the community to describe several ailments, including syphilis, anemia, and fatigue.

The participants were not informed of their syphilis diagnosis nor were they informed about the study's true purpose. Instead, they were told they were receiving free healthcare, meals, and burial insurance in exchange for participating.

Even when penicillin became the standard treatment for syphilis in 1947, the men in the study were neither informed about this development nor provided with the antibiotic. Researchers intentionally withheld treatment to observe the disease's progression.

DECEPTION:

There's no documented evidence that the men in the Tuskegee Syphilis Experiment were collectively aware that they were being deceived and subsequently made public claims about the study during its early years or even much of its duration. It's essential to understand the context and the level of manipulation involved:

The participants were deceived from the start. They were told that they were being treated for "bad blood," a local term that could refer to several conditions, including syphilis, anemia, and fatigue. The U.S. Public Health Service provided them with placebos, ineffective methods, and diagnostic procedures under the guise of "treatment." Because of this, many of the men believed they were receiving genuine healthcare.

Medical authorities, especially during the time when the study began, were highly respected. The men had little reason to doubt the intentions of the health professionals involved, especially when they were provided with certain benefits like free medical check-ups and meals during examinations.

Nurse Rivers played a pivotal role in maintaining the trust of the participants. As a Black nurse who was part of their community, she was instrumental in keeping the men involved in the study. Her relationship with the participants further ensured that they felt they were in good hands.

Many of the participants were not well-informed about syphilis, its treatments, or the broader implications of medical research. This lack of information, combined with the intentional deception by the study's conductors, made it less likely for the men to question the proceedings.

The racial dynamics of the American South in the early to mid-20th century meant that Black individuals often faced systemic racism, were marginalized, and lacked resources. Such a context might have made it even more challenging for the participants to voice concerns or seek second opinions.

EXPOSED:

The Tuskegee Syphilis Experiment became public knowledge in 1972. The unethical practices of the study were brought to national attention by Peter Buxtun, a former Public Health Service interviewer and whistleblower. Buxtun had expressed his concerns about the study to his superiors within the USPHS several times since the late 1960s, but it was only after no internal action was taken that he decided to go to the press.

Jean Heller, a reporter for the Associated Press, broke the story on July 25, 1972, revealing the details of the study to the general public. The article described how for four decades, the U.S. Public Health Service had deliberately withheld treatment from hundreds of black men with syphilis as part of a research experiment.

When the Tuskegee Syphilis Experiment was exposed by Jean Heller in 1972, the government did not deny the study's existence or its details. The facts were well-documented, and Peter Buxtun, the whistleblower, provided evidence about the experiment. Additionally, the U.S. Public Health Service, which had overseen the study, did not dispute the revelations once they were made public and shut it down.

However, in the immediate aftermath of the story breaking, some officials and representatives of the U.S. Public Health Service tried to justify or defend the study's intent and procedures, citing the research's importance or arguing that standards and norms had changed since the study began in 1932. This stance was not a denial but rather an attempt to provide context or justification, which was widely seen as insufficient and unsatisfactory given the gross ethical violations.

The media, for its part, generally reported on the story with shock and outrage. The revelations led to extensive media coverage, which played a crucial role in informing the public about the study's details and the ethical issues at stake.

The overwhelming negative reaction from the public, medical community, and media alike led to congressional hearings, which culminated in a stronger framework for the protection of human subjects in research studies and ultimately the creation of institutional review boards (IRBs) to oversee and approve research involving human participants.

CONSEQUENCES AND OUTCOMES:

Many participants of the study suffered severe health complications due to untreated syphilis, and some even died from the disease. Their families also suffered, with spouses becoming infected and children born with congenital syphilis.

In 1973, a $10 million out-of-court settlement was

reached, and the U.S. government promised to give lifetime medical benefits and burial services to all living participants. The widows of the participants were also provided with health benefits.

In 1997, President Bill Clinton formally apologized on behalf of the U.S. government to the surviving participants of the study and their families.

The experiment sowed deep distrust among many in the Black community towards the U.S. healthcare system, which still reverberates today.

Chapter 3
MK-ULTRA

PROJECT MK-ULTRA, also called the CIA mind control program, was the code name given to an illegal and clandestine program of experiments on human subjects. It was designed and undertaken by the U.S. Central Intelligence Agency (CIA) in the 1950s and 1960s. MK-ULTRA was initiated in response to perceived threats from enemy forces, especially during the Cold War. The U.S. intelligence community believed that adversaries like the Soviet Union might be using mind control techniques, so MK-ULTRA was launched to develop their own potential methods for mind control.

ORIGINS:

During the Korean War (1950-1953), there were reports of American prisoners of war (POWs) confessing to using biological weapons — allegations that were largely seen as false by U.S. authorities. These confessions and the behavior of some returning POWs raised fears of "brainwashing" techniques being employed by Communist forces.

The U.S. intelligence community became interested in the potential use of mind-altering substances as tools for interrogation, mind control, and even the manipulation of foreign leaders. This interest was heightened by reports that Soviet, Chinese, and North Korean agents were using drugs to manipulate individuals and extract information.

Officially sanctioned in 1953 by CIA Director Allen Dulles and absorbed earlier covert operations such as Project BLUEBIRD (later renamed ARTICHOKE) that aimed at discovering methods of controlling the human mind. These operations experimented with hypnosis, forced addiction, and the use of drugs like sodium amytal. MK-ULTRA expanded on the previous projects.

. . .

THE EXPERIMENTS:

MK-ULTRA involved various experiments, many of which were carried out without the knowledge or consent of the subjects. The program's focus was broad, encompassing efforts to identify drugs or techniques that could be used for mind control, information extraction, influencing foreign leaders, or even altering an individual's personality. Some of the most notable aspects and experiments under MK-ULTRA include:

- **LSD Experiments**: Unwitting subjects: The CIA administered LSD to numerous individuals without their knowledge or consent, hoping to discover a "truth serum." This included both civilians and government employees. Some of these experiments took place in safe houses in San Francisco and New York City, where the CIA would lure subjects with prostitutes and then dose them with the drug.
- **Effects on mental health**: Dr. Frank Olson, a biological warfare expert, was covertly dosed with LSD. Nine days later, he died in what was described as a suicide, jumping from a hotel window. The

circumstances of his death remain controversial.

- **Use of Other Drugs**: LSD was the most researched substance, but the CIA also experimented with other drugs, including amphetamines, barbiturates, and mescaline. These were often combined to study their synergistic effects.
- **Hypnosis**: There were attempts to induce hypnosis to create "couriers" who could deliver messages without being aware of their content or "assassins" who would carry out orders without recalling them. These goals were in line with creating a 'Manchurian Candidate'-type individual (referring to the novel and film where a person is brainwashed into becoming an unwitting assassin).
- **Subproject 68**: Led by Dr. Ewen Cameron at the Allan Memorial Institute in Canada, this infamous project involved "depatterning" and "psychic driving." Patients were exposed to repeated, high-dose electroshock treatments and prolonged drug-induced sleep, followed by forced

listening to taped messages for days on end. The intent was to "wipe" a person's memories and personality and then "reprogram" them. Many patients suffered severe long-term damage.

- **Magic Mushrooms (Psilocybin)**: The CIA was interested in the potential uses of psilocybin, the active ingredient in magic mushrooms. Dr. James C. Ketchum conducted experiments with the drug on soldiers at Edgewood Arsenal in Maryland.
- **Chemical, Biological, and Radiological Experiments**: While drug experiments are the most well-known aspect of MK-ULTRA, the program also included studies on the use of biological agents and toxins, as well as radiation exposure.
- **Institutional Involvement**: Research often took place in prestigious institutions. Some of the institutions were aware of the CIA's involvement, but many were not, with funding being channeled through front organizations. This included universities, hospitals, and pharmaceutical companies.
- **Safehouses and Surveillance**: In the 1950s and 1960s, the CIA operated

safehouses in the U.S., especially in San Francisco and New York. These were used for LSD experiments and to study sexual blackmail and surveillance technology.

The effects of these experiments varied widely. Some subjects experienced mere confusion or short-term anxiety, while others suffered severe psychological trauma, long-term mental health issues, or even death. MK-ULTRA remains a significant stain on the legacy of U.S. intelligence operations, illustrating the dangerous extremes that can result from unchecked power combined with Cold War paranoia.

EXPOSED:

Within the CIA, there were individuals who expressed discomfort or reservations about the ethical implications and efficacy of the MK-ULTRA experiments. As early as the mid-1960s, internal reviews raised questions about the project's validity and utility.

In 1973, fearing a leak and the potential for scandal, then-CIA Director Richard Helms ordered all MK-ULTRA files destroyed. While this move was intended to cover up the operation, it ironically raised suspicions when it later became apparent.

In 1974, *The New York Times* reported on the existence of the CIA's illegal domestic activities, leading to increased attention on the agency's operations. In 1975, due to a Freedom of Information Act (FOIA) request, a cache of documents related to MK-ULTRA was discovered. These were financial documents that had been spared from Helms' order of destruction because they were stored at a different location. They provided an accounting of the funds spent on the project and were a trail leading to the program's exposure.

The revelations from the FOIA discovery and the press led to a congressional investigation. In 1975, the Church Committee, led by Senator Frank Church, and the Rockefeller Commission, ordered by then-President Gerald Ford, began investigating the CIA's activities, including MK-ULTRA. Their findings were made public and brought the program to broader public awareness.

With the project's exposure, individuals who had been involved, either as researchers or subjects, began to come forward with their accounts, further solidifying the evidence of the program's existence and its controversial nature.

In the years following the exposure of MK-ULTRA, several individuals, or their families, who had been harmed by the experiments sought legal recourse, leading to court cases that further publicized details of the program.

The revelation of MK-ULTRA contributed to a more significant public awareness of the need for oversight and ethical standards in government research and operations, leading to reforms in how human research subjects are treated and protected.

FALLOUT FROM EXPOSURE:

The fallout from the revelation of MK-ULTRA was significant, both in terms of policy changes and its lasting legacy. Here's an outline of the repercussions and the long-term impact:

- The revelation that the U.S. government had conducted experiments on unwitting citizens, sometimes leading to significant harm or even death, generated substantial public shock and outrage. This was especially jarring given that the experiments included dosing individuals with LSD without their consent.
- Following the findings of the Church Committee and other investigations,

Congress implemented reforms to ensure more robust oversight of the intelligence community.
- The revelations also played a role in the establishment of the Senate Select Committee on Intelligence in 1976, ensuring more consistent oversight of intelligence activities.
- The Belmont Report, published in 1979, laid out key ethical guidelines for human subjects research, including informed consent, beneficence, and justice.
- Lawsuits were filed by some victims of MK-ULTRA experiments. In some cases, the U.S. government reached settlements or paid reparations.
- MK-ULTRA has left a lasting mark on popular culture, becoming a frequent subject in books, movies, and television series. These references often focus on themes of government conspiracy, mind control, and the misuse of psychedelic drugs.

In summary, the legacy of MK-ULTRA is

multifaceted. While it brought about essential reforms and heightened awareness of research ethics, it also left a lasting scar on the public's trust in government and became a cultural byword for government overreach and conspiracy.

HOLLYWOOD INVOLVEMENT CONSPIRACY:

The "Hollywood connection" to MK-ULTRA often refers to the idea that the entertainment industry has either been influenced by the mind control objectives of the program or has utilized its themes in various media. There are two primary facets to this connection:

MK-ULTRA in Popular Culture:

- **Films and TV Shows**: Over the years, numerous films and television shows have been inspired by or have directly referenced MK-ULTRA. The themes of mind control, government conspiracies, and the covert use of drugs have proven to be compelling subjects for narratives. Some films that touch on these themes or are inspired by MK-ULTRA include "The Manchurian Candidate" (both the original and its remake), "Jacob's Ladder," "Conspiracy Theory," and the television series "Stranger Things," where the character Eleven's backstory draws inspiration from MK-ULTRA type experiments.

- **Documentaries**: There have also been documentary films and series exploring the real history of MK-ULTRA, often weaving in interviews with survivors, archival footage, and expert commentary.

Conspiracy Theories:

• There is a subset of conspiracy theories that suggest various celebrities have been subjected to MK-ULTRA or similar "mind control" programs. Proponents of these theories often interpret celebrities' behaviors, breakdowns, or even specific symbols in their music videos or photos as "evidence" of mind control.

• Such conspiracy theories often lack concrete evidence and can verge into sensationalism. It's also important to note that conflating personal struggles or mental health issues of celebrities with covert government programs can be both misleading and harmful. However, the idea has persisted in some conspiracy-minded communities and is often lumped in with broader conspiracy theories about the entertainment industry.

To clarify, while MK-ULTRA and its themes have been explored in Hollywood in terms of storytelling, there isn't concrete evidence linking the actual program to the entertainment industry in the way some conspiracy theories suggest. As with all conspiracy theories, it's crucial to approach such claims with skepticism and discernment and to differentiate between fictional depictions and real-world evidence…..but then again, it could be true as we all know.

Chapter 4
COINTELPRO

THE COUNTER INTELLIGENCE PROGRAM, commonly known as COINTELPRO, was a covert FBI initiative that targeted perceived "subversive" groups within the United States. Initiated in 1956, its express purpose was to "disrupt, misdirect, discredit, or otherwise neutralize" political organizations and individuals deemed threats to the established social order.

ORIGIN:

By the mid-1950s, the civil rights movement was gaining momentum. Simultaneously, Cold War tensions were heightening fears about communism. Hoover perceived the civil rights movement, especially its leaders like Martin Luther King Jr., as susceptible to communist influence. The confluence of these events set the stage for COINTELPRO.

Under the stewardship of its long-time director, J. Edgar Hoover, the FBI had grown increasingly alarmed by the burgeoning civil rights movement, fearing it was under the influence of communists or other external agitators. The bureau was particularly concerned about the potential for a "Black messiah" — a charismatic leader who could unify and electrify the civil rights and Black nationalist movements. Dr. Martin Luther King Jr., Malcolm X, and the Black Panther Party were among the program's most notable targets.

But COINTELPRO wasn't just about racial matters. Over time, its net widened to include anti-Vietnam War activists, feminist organizations, Native American groups, and even the Puerto Rican independence movement.

The first official COINTELPRO operation, started in 1956, was titled "COINTELPRO - Communist Party, USA (CPUSA)" and aimed to disrupt the Communist Party's operations in the U.S. It relied on infiltration, surveillance, and the spreading of misinformation.

By the 1960s, the program expanded its focus beyond the Communist Party. It began to target other groups seen as potential threats to the "existing social and political order." This encompassed the civil rights movement, Black nationalist groups, feminist organizations, Puerto Rican independence activists, and anti-Vietnam War protestors, among others.

Director Hoover had a particular animus towards Dr. Martin Luther King Jr. and the Black Panther Party. Under COINTELPRO, both King and the Panthers became significant targets. Hoover's personal biases significantly influenced the direction and intensity of the program.

METHODS AND TACTICS:

To carry out COINTELPRO's objectives, the FBI used a range of covert tactics:

- **Informants**: The FBI placed informants within targeted groups to gather information and, in some cases, to sow discord.
- **Forgeries**: False communications were created to instigate disputes between different organizations or within the same group.

- **Surveillance**: This ranged from phone taps to following individuals. Dr. King was under almost constant surveillance during the last years of his life.
- **Negative Publicity**: The FBI provided information (sometimes false) to the media to discredit individuals or organizations in the public eye.
- **Harassment and Intimidation**: This included sending anonymous letters, often with threats or false information, to create paranoia or fear.

The inception of COINTELPRO was, in essence, the institutional manifestation of deep-seated fears and prejudices. By covertly working against groups advocating for societal change, the program was an attempt by the federal government to maintain a certain status quo. Over time, however, as its tactics became more extreme and its targets more diverse, COINTELPRO morphed into a symbol of government overreach and paranoia.

EXPOSURE:

The catalyst for the exposure of COINTELPRO

was a break-in at a small FBI office in Media, Pennsylvania.

A group of activists, some of whom had previously protested the Vietnam War, became convinced that the FBI was suppressing the rights of anti-war protesters and civil rights workers. They decided to break into an FBI office to search for evidence. Their aim was to unearth documentation of any federal surveillance or intimidation tactics. They chose the Media office, suspecting a smaller location would hold important documents but be less guarded than a major city office.

On March 8, 1971, while much of the country was distracted by the Muhammad Ali-Joe Frazier fight, the group successfully broke into the Media FBI office. They managed to steal several files.

As the activists sifted through the stolen documents, they found evidence of the FBI's covert actions against civil rights leaders, anti-war activists, and other groups. Among the files was a document with a reference to "COINTELPRO," a term that was unfamiliar to the public at that time.

Recognizing the significance of their discovery, the activists decided to share the documents with the press. They sent copies of the files to major newspapers, including The Washington Post, which was one of the first to report on the contents.

The initial news stories about the stolen documents led to further investigations by journalists, activists, and eventually Congress:

Once COINTELPRO's existence became public knowledge, investigative journalists played a pivotal role in unraveling the scope of its activities. Over time, articles exposed various covert operations and targeted individuals.

In the wake of these revelations, and coupled with other concerns about intelligence agency overreach (e.g., the Watergate scandal), a Senate committee was formed to investigate the actions of U.S. intelligence agencies. Known as the Church Committee, after its chairman Senator Frank Church, this committee delved into the actions of the FBI, CIA, and other agencies. During its investigations, the committee unveiled many of the tactics and targets of COINTELPRO.

COINTELPRO was officially terminated in 1971, with the break-in and its subsequent exposure being a significant factor in its end.

FALLOUT:

The exposure of COINTELPRO had profound implications for the FBI, the U.S. government, and the trust of the American people in their institutions. Here's a look at the immediate and lasting fallout:

The FBI faced significant criticism and backlash. J. Edgar Hoover's tactics, which had once been seen by many as essential for national security, were now viewed as an abuse of power. The revelations severely tarnished the bureau's image, portraying it as an agency that had overstepped its bounds, violated the Constitution, and infringed on the rights of American citizens.

Attorney General Edward Levi established new guidelines in 1976 to govern FBI domestic operations, ensuring more stringent oversight and control over the agency's domestic intelligence activities.

While COINTELPRO had long-term negative effects on many of the groups it targeted, its exposure also led to greater solidarity among them. Many activists became even more resolute in their efforts, and they were now armed with concrete evidence of government overreach and misconduct.

The revelations added to the growing mistrust of the U.S. government. For many, COINTELPRO epitomized the dangers of unchecked governmental power.

There was recognition within the FBI that the agency needed to evolve. The bureau took steps to modernize its operations, improve its public image, and ensure that its activities were transparent and within the rule of law. This involved not only policy changes but also efforts to shift the agency's internal culture.

Some individuals targeted by COINTELPRO sought legal redress. This led to several lawsuits against the FBI and the U.S. government. In some cases, the government settled and provided compensation.

COINTELPRO's exposure heightened public awareness about the importance of checks and balances, the rule of law, and the potential for government abuse. It spurred a generation of activists and watchdog groups to be more vigilant in holding the government accountable.

In essence, the fallout from COINTELPRO's exposure was multifaceted, leading to reforms, increased skepticism of governmental power, and a reinforced commitment among activists and civil rights proponents. It stands as a stark reminder of the need for transparency, accountability, and public oversight in democratic societies.

Knowing that the FBI conducted itself in such a dishonest and corrupt way, can we be sure they're still not doing so with groups they don't like politically?

Chapter 5
OPERATION NORTHWOODS

IN THE EARLY 1960S, tensions between the U.S. and Cuba were at an all-time high. Following Fidel Castro's rise to power and the establishment of a communist regime in Cuba, the U.S. sought ways to counteract or eliminate this perceived threat close to its borders.

Operation Northwoods was conceived against this backdrop of heightened Cold War tension and the U.S.'s determination to contain or roll back communism in its own hemisphere. Specifically, it was part of the broader strategy to justify military intervention in Cuba and oust Castro.

The plan was drafted by the U.S. Department of Defense and the Joint Chiefs of Staff. It outlined a series of proposed actions, including covert operations and false flag operations, to create the appearance of Cuban aggression against the U.S. or its interests, which would then be used as a pretext for military intervention.

DETAILS OF THE PLAN:

1. False Flag Operations: These are covert operations designed to deceive the public into thinking that actions were carried out by entities other than those who actually planned and executed them. Operation Northwoods proposed actions that would appear to be of Cuban origin, including:

- Attacks on U.S. military bases.
- Terror campaigns in U.S. cities.
- Hi-jacking of planes.
- Attacks on U.S. ships.
- Creating a "Cuban" terrorist group in the U.S.

2. **Plausible Deniability**: The plan stressed that the operations should be conducted in a way that the U.S. could deny any involvement.

3. No Real Harm: While some of the proposals involved the potential for real harm or even fatalities, others suggested using fake operations, such as mock funerals or simulated attacks.

ARCHITECTS OF THE PLAN:

Operation Northwoods was developed by high-ranking military officials within the U.S. Department of Defense and the Joint Chiefs of Staff. Some of the notable individuals involved in the proposal included:

- Gen. Lyman L. Lemnitzer: He was the Chairman of the Joint Chiefs of Staff at the time. Lemnitzer approved the Northwoods proposal and presented it to Secretary of Defense Robert McNamara. However, McNamara rejected it, and it's believed that Lemnitzer's support for such covert activities like Northwoods played a role in President Kennedy's decision not to reappoint him as Chairman.

- Brig. Gen. William H. Craig: He was the Chief of the Cuba Project, and the Northwoods document was presented by him to the Joint Chiefs of Staff.

- Gen. Earle G. Wheeler: He later replaced Lemnitzer as Chairman of the Joint Chiefs of Staff, but at the time of Northwoods, he was the Chief of Staff of the Army. Wheeler, along with the other service chiefs, would have been privy to and approved the proposal.

- The other Joint Chiefs of Staff members at the time also would have known about and given their approval to the proposal. This includes the chiefs of the Army, Navy, Air Force, and Marine Corps.

It's important to note that while these high-ranking military officials approved the proposal, it was ultimately rejected at the higher civilian leadership level by Secretary of Defense Robert McNamara. There's no concrete evidence that President John F. Kennedy was ever made aware of the plan.

EXPOSURE:

Operation Northwoods was never approved or carried out. President John F. Kennedy, who was briefed on the proposal, rejected it. The existence of the plan remained classified and out of public view for decades.

It wasn't until 2001, during the release of documents related to the assassination of President Kennedy, that Operation Northwoods was publicly disclosed. The release of these documents was spearheaded by the Assassination Records Review Board, a civilian panel established by Congress to collate and release information related to Kennedy's assassination.

The revelation was covered in major media outlets, and James Bamford, a journalist specializing in national security issues, highlighted the operation in his book "Body of Secrets."

FALLOUT:

Once the details of Operation Northwoods became public, there was significant outcry and shock that U.S. military leaders had proposed such actions, even if they were never approved or executed.

The revelation also led to discussions and debates about the integrity and ethics of some military leaders during the Cold War era.

Operation Northwoods fueled various conspiracy theories, as it provided a concrete example of a high-level government plan to deceive and manipulate the public. Some used it to argue that other conspiracy theories might have validity. (Of course they do!)

For historians and political analysts, the plan provided a lens into the intense Cold War mindset and the lengths to which some officials considered going to achieve geopolitical aims.

While Operation Northwoods never moved beyond the proposal stage, its disclosure decades later provided a sobering look into the strategies contemplated during the most intense periods of the Cold War. The knowledge of its existence remains a cautionary tale about unchecked power and the importance of ethical considerations, even in the face of geopolitical challenges.

It also proved to many skeptics that the government will go to great lengths, including false flags operations and the killing of Americans, to ensure their agenda is pushed through. Can you think of any recent events that might be false flags?

PUBLISHER'S EXCERPT
TALES OF TERROR: VOLUME 1

FOLLOWED BY EVIL

It's no secret that a lot of people like to retreat into the woods to escape the rigors of everyday life and reality in general. It's peaceful out there in the middle of mother nature and up until I was about fifteen years old, I felt the same way about it. However, once I had the experience I did while out camping with my best friend back in 1973, I have never been the same again. I also haven't ever gone into the woods again, for the most part, at night or even when it was dusk. Whatever we saw out there stayed with us and it's something that, though I've never physically seen it again, it has haunted my nightmares in all the years since. My best friend back then is still my best friend today and she and I share that evil experience and she feels the same way as I do about it. She also has nightmares and has avoided the woods at night at all costs ever since. No one believed us back then but for the most part, when we tell the story nowadays, people seem to at least give us the benefit of the doubt. We didn't do drugs or drink at all and in fact we weren't popular with most of the other kids in our school at the time because of our "goody goody" ways. That was neither here nor there for us and we enjoyed each other's company, as we still do. Here is the story of what happened to us and what could happen to you if you aren't careful and find yourself messing around with things you couldn't possibly understand.

Our families were friends as well so a lot of the time we would all vacation together. My best friend, Emily, had an older brother who was the same age as my own older brother, and she had one younger sister. Our mothers and fathers had all gone to high school together, the same high school we attended, in the same small town. We even had some of the same teachers as they did. I know that's wild when you really think about it, but it wasn't that uncommon back in those days. We grew up in rural Kentucky surrounded by roads that seemed to go on for miles and miles and lead to nowhere. Emily and I would spend hours walking along those roads and hanging out in the woods that surrounded them. There wouldn't be a house in sight, no signs of normal civilization and we could go hours without seeing or hearing another human being. She and I always had interests that other people considered bizarre and that our very religious parents were horrified by. We thought it was all in good fun, as we learned new ways to try and divine our futures and connect with the spirit world. We knew our parents had an end of the school year camping trip planned for all of us and we decided it was a good idea to sneak a Ouija board in with our stuff. The way we ended up with that board is another story altogether, but it isn't too relevant to the encounter we ended up having so I will just say we stole it from a shop near our home. The owner of the shop was said to be a devil worshiper and a witch, but not a good one. She was a mean old woman who seemed to hate kids our age and getting it out of the store was a mission in and of itself. However, I often wonder now if the old hag knew all along what we were doing and what we had done, and if it was her doing, what happened to us.

We all set off in a campervan, but we weren't going to all be staying in it together. It was big enough for the twelve-hour drive and seven people, but it wouldn't sleep all of us. Me and Emily and both of our brothers would sleep outside with our parents and her baby sister inside. It was the first year the adults would be sleeping inside and allowing us kids to sleep on the outside and we were excited. Our older brothers were typical for that time, and they mocked and picked on us relentlessly so she and I had a plan that we thought would work and allow us the time, space, and privacy we needed to use the pilfered board. Eventually we got to the campsite and spent the whole night hanging out by the fire, eating, and having a great time with our families. Eventually though it was time to go to sleep and that's when Emily and I enacted our plan. We picked a fight with our brothers and then begged our parents to let us go further into the woods, just a little bit, so we could have some privacy overnight. They eventually relented because they knew our brothers would be right there within ear shot. Also, they knew no matter how much we fought they wouldn't let anything happen to us should they hear us screaming or otherwise in some distress. I could tell our moms were nervous, but they let us go and Emily and I walked for about five minutes deeper into the woods. We only needed it to be far enough away that the boys wouldn't hear our whispers or notice the tealight candles we planned on lighting during our Ouija board session.

Emily and I had some whispered conversations about how to use the board. We had recently watched a horror movie that had a Ouija board in it, and everyone died at the end except one person. You would think that would have deterred us from ever even going near one, but you would be wrong, and it only made us want to try one even more. Back in the early seventies, where we come from, it was considered evil and demonic to want to speak with the dead, but Emily and I were just planning on asking it basic and somewhat silly questions about boys we liked and teachers we didn't like, stuff like that. We weren't taking it seriously at all and that was our first, worst and biggest mistake. As soon as we no longer heard our brothers, we took the board and the candles out. We were both sitting on our sleeping bags across from one another and we had the board in the middle. The only candles we had were four little, half used tea lights that we had taken from my mother's office. We lit the candles, and the air was still so they weren't immediately going out or anything. One strange thing we did notice is that as soon as our fingers hit the planchette, the forest seemed to go very quiet, and very still, suddenly. It freaked us out a little bit but again, it wasn't something that we were going to allow to deter us. We were frightened but excited and we giggled the whole time. At first, we asked if anyone was there, and the planchette immediately moved to the word "goodbye." That happened three times, but we didn't take the hint and continued trying to get something to communicate with us. We asked for the fourth time if anyone was there and the planchette moved to "yes." I knew Emily wasn't moving it and she knew that I wasn't, and we both immediately took our hands off the board. We were scared and both of us had a bad feeling. Still though, we pressed on. After a few minutes of establishing a connection, a spirit came through that claimed to be my grandfather. He had recently passed, and it had been very hard on me. He and I were super close and losing him had devastated me. I was in tears as I asked questions that only he would know the answers to and every single time the board, which I thought my grandfather was communicating with me through from beyond the grave, knew all the right answers.

This went on for about five minutes, the exchange with my "grandfather." Suddenly things started to get very scary. A very strong gust of wind came out of nowhere in the otherwise calm and windless night. It didn't only blow the candles out completely, but it sent two of them flying into the woods like they were made of feathers instead of hard wax and a metal base. At the same time, the planchette flew off the board and hit a nearby tree. We heard growling coming from somewhere in the woods, very close to us, right when the wind stopped blowing and the candles and planchette had landed. We didn't scream because honestly at that point we were more scared of our families catching us than we were of what we thought could have just been a little series of strange coincidences. We were both shaking and once the growling stopped, I started to giggle. I giggled and laughed a lot when I was very nervous and didn't know what else to do. Emily was giggling too, but I think she was doing it more to try and calm herself down. We decided to collect the candles and the planchette and hide the board in the woods. We knew we were supposed to get it to say "goodbye" before stopping the session with it, but we were inexperienced and decided to just ditch the board in the woods and get rid of the candles. I got up to collect the candles and told Emily to collect the board and planchette. She was reluctant and instead said she would keep watch to make sure no one from our families was coming close to us so that we didn't get caught. I hadn't thought of that and so I agreed to just collect everything and put it all into my bag. We were going to walk further into the woods, just a little bit, and hide everything. When we left to go home, we would just leave it there. Whatever we conjured that night, which wasn't my dearly departed grandfather, had other plans for us though.

I told Emily to keep watch while I walked and hid everything. She agreed and was happy not to have to go further into the woods or even touch that board again. We were both filled with terror and instant regret about what we had done. We would make sure we prayed later to find forgiveness because we also felt very guilty for using the spirit board. That's what we called it back then by the way, a spirit board. I felt like I was being followed the entire time I was looking with my flashlight for a place to put the board and candles where we wouldn't accidentally come across it when walking around with our parents and siblings. I heard a growling sound and when I turned to look there were two sets of red eyes peering at me from behind the trees. I screamed and dropped everything right there where I stood. I ran back to tell Emily what had happened. I felt like something was running behind me the entire way and I could hear the growling right next to my ear as though whatever it was, it was almost right on top of me. Emily and I took a long time to calm down and we tried to pray but kept being scared by the growling and losing our concentration. We looked around and all we saw were the two sets of red eyes looking at us, but we didn't see what was attached to them at first. Eventually, I think from adrenaline alone, we both passed out. I woke up to Emily screaming and when I looked over at her she was being dragged around in her sleeping bag. I will never forget the look of terror in her eyes and on her face at that moment. I looked up and suddenly there was a gigantic shadow figure hovering over me as I laid there, helpless to help either myself or my friend. I tried to scream but nothing would come out. The entity had red eyes that exuded evil and malicious intent. It smelled like someone was burning their trash nearby, but I knew it was the entity itself. It had a hood over its head. Eventually a small shriek escaped my throat, and I was able to move again. I jumped up and ran over to my best friend and asked if she was okay. She said that she was but we both had scratches all over our legs and arms.

She had tears in her sleeping bag as if a grizzly bear had swiped it or something. We didn't know what to do and were shocked when no one came running at the sounds of our screaming.

We put her sleeping bag back across from mine and just sat there, crying, and trying to comfort one another. Our scratches were bleeding a little bit, and later we saw they were only scrapes. As we sat there, we heard growling and the wind picked up again. Whatever was out there wasn't done with us yet. Two shadow beings, both about twelve or thirteen feet tall with red eyes and a shadowy hood walked out of the wilderness beyond where we were sitting. The hoods dropped from their heads and what we saw were the most grotesque and hideous beings or creatures we had ever seen. Their skin seemed like it was burning off their faces. They had green fangs for teeth and huge, puss filled globs all over their faces. They were slowly floating towards us, and it was almost like we were in one of the terrifying but very cheesy horror movies we loved to watch so much. It didn't take either one of us any consideration and we got up and ran to the campervan to tell our parents what had happened. In typical style of religious parents, they were only focused on the fact we had used the board and not anything else that we had been through. We got in so much trouble and once we were back home, we were both grounded for the entire summer. We also underwent something like an exorcism at church and honestly, I think that's what saved us from being haunted, hunted and overtaken by those two demons from hell that either dwelt in those woods already or who we summoned from the board. Maybe it was a little bit of both.

TALES OF TERROR: VOLUME 1

PUBLISHER'S EXCERPT 2
STALKED: TERRIFYING TRUE CRIME STORIES: VOLUME 1

THE FLASH DRIVE

Around 6 1/2 years ago, I resided alone in a quaint little house in a small town nestled far away from the bustling region of Auckland, New Zealand. The peacefulness of my surroundings was shattered one fateful morning when an incident occurred that would forever remain etched in my memory as one of the most terrifying experiences of my life.

It all began when I woke up and decided to venture out to buy groceries I had forgotten to purchase from the local market, which opened every day at 8:30 am, even on weekdays. As I opened my front door, ready to embark on my errand, I was greeted by an unexpected sight - lying right in the center of my doorstep was a small, inconspicuous USB flash drive. It was so tiny that I nearly stepped on it in my surprise.

Confused and suspicious, I quickly glanced around, half-expecting someone to jump out and reveal themselves as the prankster behind this peculiar occurrence. However, the outside of my house remained eerily silent, leaving me with a flood of questions swirling in my mind. Who could have left the USB drive there, and for what purpose? It appeared to be a generic device with no label or markings, leaving me to wonder why someone would take the time to walk up to my house and place it on my doorstep.

Despite my misgivings, curiosity got the better of me, and I decided to bring the USB drive inside and plug it into my computer. The contents of the device turned out to be nothing but pictures - dozens of them filling every available space. I proceeded to open the first picture and began clicking through them in order.

The initial images were of familiar places around town, scenes I often passed by during my morning strolls. However, my heart skipped a beat when I came across the fourth picture. It captured the busiest street in our town, and amidst the crowd, there I was, going about my business during a grocery run for a BBQ the day before.

At first, I dismissed it as mere coincidence, considering it was a small town where everyone frequently crossed paths. But as I clicked through the next image, taken on the same day, I realized the photographer had been closer to me than before. This time, it seemed too close for comfort. I found myself in several more pictures taken on different occasions and locations around town, but what came next chilled me to the bone.

The next set of pictures featured my house, taken from outside at nighttime when the living-room light was on. Clicking through the images, I noticed they grew increasingly closer and more detailed. Through the living-room window, I could see myself sitting on the couch with my phone, and it was evident the picture had been taken the night before, right after I had taken a shower. I had no clue that someone had been watching me from outside my home. The intruder didn't even need to use the camera's flash, taking advantage of the contrast between the bright interior and the dark exterior.

As I continued clicking through the images, my heart pounded with fear and confusion. There were more pictures of me inside my house, captured from just outside my window. The intruder had managed to take photographs of me inside all my rooms, including my bedroom, where I slept peacefully, completely unaware of the person lurking outside.

The realization hit me like a bolt of lightning - this individual had not only invaded my privacy but had also come inside my house during the night, taking pictures of every corner. The unnerving feeling intensified as I saw images of my living room and other spaces, all empty and devoid of light, suggesting they had been taken after I had gone to bed.

The final pictures were of me fast asleep in my bed, blissfully unaware of the intruder's presence. The last image contained a chilling handwritten note framed in closeup, with a simple yet haunting message: "Never hide a spare key under your doormat."

Fearful and paranoid about my safety, I wasted no time in packing my belongings and moving to a new house, hoping to leave this terrifying chapter behind.

To this day, the questions remain unanswered, leaving me to wonder who the perpetrator was and what their motives truly were. The incident serves as a constant reminder to never underestimate the importance of security and the potential dangers that may lurk in the shadows, even in the most serene of surroundings.

STALKED: VOLUME 1

Chapter 6
THE HEART ATTACK GUN

THE COLD WAR produced many rumors and speculations about the existence of covert assassination tools that could be used by intelligence agencies to eliminate targets discreetly. One such weapon rumored during the Cold War was simply called, The Heart Attack Gun. The specifics about this weapon and its exact mechanism weren't widely known until they were officially disclosed during Senate Hearings in the 1970s.

ORIGIN:

The Heart Attack Gun is a product of the Cold War era, during which covert operations, espionage, and counter-intelligence played significant roles for both the United States and the Soviet Union. While the exact genesis and timeline of the weapon's development aren't fully documented in the public record, here's what we do know:

-Motive: The period after World War II and into the latter half of the 20th century was marked by intense rivalry between the U.S. and the USSR. Espionage and counter-espionage operations were vital components of this rivalry, leading to an arms race not just in nuclear capability but also in intelligence and covert operation tools.

The Central Intelligence Agency (CIA) was at the forefront of many covert operations during this era. The agency actively pursued avenues to gain advantages over adversaries, including the development of specialized weapons for espionage and potential assassinations.

- Development: The primary challenge was to create a weapon that could eliminate a target without drawing attention or leaving obvious traces that could be tied back to an assassination. The weapon would need to be silent, effective, and leave a cause of death that would likely not raise suspicions. The Heart Attack Gun was developed to meet this challenge. By using a frozen dart filled with a potent toxin derived from shellfish, the weapon could ensure that the victim would appear to die from natural causes, specifically a heart attack.

- Design and Mechanism:

Resembling a pistol, the weapon was unremarkable in design. It was specifically crafted to be silent, not drawing attention to its operation.

The primary element was a dart, minute in size and constructed of ice. Within this frozen projectile was a small amount of shellfish toxin.

When fired, the dart could penetrate clothing and ultimately enter the target's body, leaving just a pin-sized red dot, akin to a mosquito bite. The absence of noise upon firing and the minor, inconspicuous wound made it unlikely that the target would notice the attack.

The shellfish toxin within the dart was potent enough to cause rapid heart failure. Once introduced into the body, it would act quickly, leading the target to suffer what appeared to be a natural heart attack.

- Toxin Details:

The poison used was derived from shellfish and was a potent neurotoxin.

Upon entering the bloodstream, it could cause a sudden cardiac arrest.

The toxin breaks down quickly in the body, and given the period (the 1970s), it would have been challenging to detect during an autopsy, especially if the investigators were not specifically looking for it.

EXPOSURE:

The Heart Attack Gun was revealed to the public during the Church Committee hearings in 1975. The Church Committee, named after its chairman, Senator Frank Church, was established by the U.S. Senate to investigate abuses by U.S. intelligence agencies, including the Central Intelligence Agency (CIA), Federal Bureau of Investigation (FBI), and the National Security Agency (NSA).

Amidst concerns about domestic surveillance, assassination plots, and other unauthorized and potentially illegal activities by U.S. intelligence agencies, the Church Committee was tasked with investigating and providing a comprehensive report on these matters.

During one of the sessions in 1975, the Heart Attack Gun was presented. The CIA displayed this weapon, explaining its intended use and functionality. Officials from the CIA demonstrated the pistol, explaining that it fired a dart made of frozen water and shellfish toxin. Once inside the target, the dart would melt, leaving only a tiny red dot on the skin, while the toxin itself would cause a heart attack in the victim.

. . .

AFTERMATH:

While the Church Committee's revelations about the Heart Attack Gun were sensational, they were part of broader disclosures about U.S. intelligence activities that ranged from assassination plots against foreign leaders to domestic surveillance programs against American citizens.

The disclosure of such a weapon stunned many in the public. It became emblematic of the cloak-and-dagger operations of the intelligence agencies and the lengths they might go for covert actions.

The hearings led to significant reforms in how U.S. intelligence agencies operated and increased oversight from Congress.

In popular culture and among conspiracy theorists, the Heart Attack Gun remains a topic of interest and speculation, often cited as evidence of the capabilities of intelligence agencies to carry out covert and untraceable assassinations.

Chapter 7
OPERATION SNOW WHITE

OPERATION SNOW WHITE is one of the largest infiltrations of the U.S. government in history that we know of. Orchestrated by the Church of Scientology during the 1970s, its primary goal was to purge unfavorable records about Scientology and its founder, L. Ron Hubbard.

BACKGROUND:

The Church of Scientology had been facing various challenges and investigations by different government agencies, mainly due to allegations of practicing medicine without a license, among other issues. Additionally, there were many documents within governmental archives that the Church felt were false and which painted the organization and L. Ron Hubbard in a negative light.

DETAILS:

The objective of the operation aimed to identify and correct perceived injustices and "false reports" about Scientology and L. Ron Hubbard within government agencies, primarily in the U.S., but it extended to other countries as well.

The Church of Scientology operatives, belonging to the Church's Guardian's Office, infiltrated numerous government agencies, such as the IRS. They wiretapped offices, stole documents, and eavesdropped on government officials.

By the Church's accounts, the operation included over 5,000 covert agents who infiltrated over 136 government agencies, foreign embassies, and consulates, as well as prominent private organizations and the homes of selected private individuals.

PEOPLE INVOLVED:

Operation Snow White was orchestrated by the Church of Scientology's Guardian's Office. Several members of this office were involved, but a few played particularly key roles:

- **Mary Sue Hubbard**: As the third wife of L. Ron Hubbard (founder of Scientology), Mary Sue Hubbard was the most high-profile figure implicated in Operation Snow White. She held the post of "Controller" and supervised the Guardian's Office, which carried out the operation. Mary Sue was deeply involved in directing the actions of the Church's agents and was eventually convicted and sentenced to prison for her role in the conspiracy.
- **Jane Kember**: As the Guardian Worldwide for the Church, Kember was another senior figure in the Guardian's Office and was based in England. She was one of the individuals convicted in connection with Operation Snow White for her involvement in directing and coordinating activities.
- **Morris "Mo" Budlong**: As the Deputy Guardian for Information Worldwide, Budlong was directly under Kember and played an instrumental role in the

operation. He was also among those convicted.
- **Gerald Wolfe**: Wolfe was one of the operatives who infiltrated the IRS. He was caught in the act of theft, leading to the FBI's investigation and the subsequent unraveling of the broader operation.
- **Michael Meisner**: Initially a co-conspirator, Meisner infiltrated various U.S. government agencies. He later became a key whistleblower, cooperating with the FBI and providing crucial information that led to raids on Scientology offices and the discovery of evidence implicating the Church in the operation.
- **L. Ron Hubbard**: While not directly implicated in the day-to-day operations of Snow White, L. Ron Hubbard, the founder of the Church of Scientology, was named as an "unindicted co-conspirator" in the case. Some believe he was aware of, and possibly directed, the activities of the Guardian's Office. However, he was not formally charged.

Several other individuals from the Guardian's

Office were involved in carrying out the operation, but the figures mentioned above are among the most notable due to their high-ranking positions within the Church or their direct involvement in the infiltration and theft of documents.

EXPOSURE:

Operation Snow White became known largely due to mistakes made by the Church's operatives, followed by an FBI investigation and subsequent raids that uncovered extensive evidence of the operation. Here's a brief sequence of how the operation unraveled:

- **Mistakes and Suspicion**: The first cracks in the operation appeared when Gerald Wolfe, an operative working for the Church of Scientology, was caught in the act of unauthorized access at the IRS in 1976. This raised suspicions, and authorities began to monitor his activities.

- **Michael Meisner's Detention and Escape**: Michael Meisner, another key operative involved in the operation, was arrested in connection with the theft of government documents. The Church of Scientology subsequently kept Meisner under watch in a Church building to prevent him from revealing details of the operation to law enforcement. However, Meisner managed to escape and soon began cooperating with the authorities.

- **FBI Investigation**: With Meisner's cooperation, the FBI gained valuable insights into the extent of the Church's infiltration and illegal activities within various U.S. government agencies. This information paved the way for what would come next.

- **FBI Raids**: In 1977, armed with information from their investigations and Meisner's testimonies, the FBI conducted extensive raids on Church of Scientology offices in Los Angeles and Washington, D.C. During these raids, the FBI seized tens of thousands of documents that revealed the full scope of Operation Snow White. These documents not only showed evidence of infiltrations and theft but also outlined plans for the operation.

- **Public Exposure**: Following the FBI raids and the subsequent trials, details about Operation Snow White became public knowledge, leading to widespread media coverage and public scrutiny. The seized documents played a crucial role in the prosecution of Church officials involved in the operation.

FALLOUT:

The fallout from Operation Snow White was significant for both the Church of Scientology and the individuals directly involved. Here are some of the major consequences:

- **Criminal Convictions**: Eleven high-ranking members of the Church of Scientology's Guardian's Office were convicted of charges related to the conspiracy. Most notably, Mary Sue Hubbard, the wife of Scientology's founder L. Ron Hubbard, was sentenced to five years in prison but served only a portion of that time. Others convicted included senior Church officials Jane Kember and Morris "Mo" Budlong.

- **Disbandment of the Guardian's Office**: As a response to the scandal and the criminal activities it had undertaken, the Guardian's Office was disbanded by the Church. It was replaced by the Office of Special Affairs (OSA), which handles public relations, legal affairs, and other matters for the Church.

- **Increased Scrutiny and Distrust**: The revelations from Operation Snow White significantly tarnished the public image of the Church of Scientology. The Church's involvement in illegal infiltrations and theft from U.S. government offices led to increased public and governmental scrutiny, deepening the mistrust many had toward the organization.

- **Internal Reforms**: The Church of Scientology declared that those involved in the illegal activities of

Operation Snow White had been purged from the organization. They presented the scandal as the result of actions by rogue members, even though those involved were high-ranking officials.

L. Ron Hubbard's Role and Secrecy: While L. Ron Hubbard was named as an "unindicted co-conspirator" in the case, he was not formally charged. However, the scandal further shrouded him in controversy. In the years following the exposure of Operation Snow White, Hubbard became increasingly reclusive, going into seclusion until his death in 1986.

- Strained Relations with the U.S. Government: The Church of Scientology's relationship with the U.S. government, which was already tense due to issues like tax exemption status, was further strained. The operation and its exposure highlighted the lengths to which the Church was willing to go in its battles against perceived enemies, making any negotiations or interactions with governmental bodies more contentious.

- Fuel for Critics: The details and scale of Operation Snow White provided critics of the Church with significant ammunition. The operation is often cited in discussions about the Church's history of dealing with its critics and perceived adversaries.

In the years since Operation Snow White, the

Church of Scientology has sought to move past the scandal, emphasizing its charitable works and religious teachings. However, the operation remains one of the most significant and controversial events in the Church's history.

Operation Snow White also shows how one private organization can make a foothold inside the government in order to manipulate. Who believes the Church of Scientology was the only organization who has done this or is currently doing this? I dare say our government has nefarious players in its ranks today.

Chapter 8
OPERATION PAPERCLIP

OPERATION PAPERCLIP WAS a covert program initiated by the U.S. Office of Strategic Services (OSS) and later executed by the Joint Intelligence Objectives Agency (JIOA) after World War II. Its primary objective was to recruit and bring to the United States German scientists, engineers, and technicians (some who had been Nazis) to gain a competitive advantage in the Cold War and the ongoing space race. The name "Paperclip" comes from the paperclips used to attach the scientists' new profiles onto their U.S. personnel files.

ORIGINS:

As the Allies advanced into Germany near the end of World War II, they began to discover a wealth of scientific data and advanced technology. This was particularly evident in sectors like rocketry, jet propulsion, synthetic rubber, and chemical warfare.

Both the Western Allies (mainly the U.S. and the UK) and the Soviets recognized the immense strategic value in acquiring German scientific knowledge and expertise. This led to a scramble to identify, capture, and recruit key German scientists, engineers, and technicians before the other side could.

Before Operation Paperclip was formally initiated, there were other efforts. For instance, the U.S. Office of Strategic Services (OSS) ran **Operation Overcast**, primarily aimed at the capture and interrogation of German personnel who could be useful in the post-war period.

Initially, the U.S. aimed at debriefing these scientists and sending them back. However, the realization of their value in the burgeoning Cold War conflict against the Soviet Union shifted the objective towards permanent relocation to the U.S.

IMPLEMENTATION:

President Harry S. Truman authorized Operation

Paperclip in August 1945, though he explicitly excluded anyone found "to have been a member of the Nazi Party, and more than a nominal participant in its activities, or an active supporter of Nazi militarism." This directive, however, was often overlooked or worked around to ensure that the U.S. got the expertise it wanted.

Parallel to the American efforts, the Soviet Union had its own operation known as "Osoaviakhim." During this operation, they forcibly relocated more than 2,200 German specialists and their families to the Soviet Union to work on various projects.

The JIOA (Joint Intelligence Objectives Agency), which took over from the OSS, was the primary agency responsible for identifying, recruiting, and relocating German scientists to the U.S. They worked in collaboration with the U.S. Army and other government agencies.

Given Truman's directives, the backgrounds of several scientists were cleaned up or whitewashed to omit or downplay their Nazi Party affiliations or any war crimes. This "denazification" of records was done to bypass the restrictions and ensure that the selected individuals could work in the U.S. without too much public or governmental scrutiny.

In essence, the origins of Operation Paperclip were

rooted in the strategic necessities of the time. The Cold War was rapidly replacing WWII's clear-cut alliances, and the U.S. wanted every advantage it could get in its new rivalry against the Soviet Union. The expertise of these German scientists was seen as a ticket to dominance in crucial areas of technology, research, and warfare.

MAJOR PLAYERS:
U.S. Entities and Figures:
- **Office of Strategic Services (OSS)**: The predecessor to the CIA, the OSS initially oversaw the efforts to recruit German scientists before the program was formally named Operation Paperclip.
- **Joint Intelligence Objectives Agency (JIOA)**: The main U.S. agency responsible for executing Operation Paperclip, they managed the recruitment, transportation, and placement of German scientists in the U.S.
- **Major General Hugh Knerr**: An advocate of importing German scientists to the U.S., he was instrumental in the establishment and functioning of Operation Paperclip.
- **U.S. Army**: Played a significant role in the identification, interrogation, and hiring of German experts,

especially those with expertise in rocketry and ballistic missiles.

- **U.S. Air Force**: They were particularly interested in German advances in jet propulsion and aviation technologies.

German Figures:

- **Wernher von Braun**: Arguably the most famous scientist recruited through Operation Paperclip. He had been the technical director of the Peenemünde V-2 rocket research center in Nazi Germany. In the U.S., von Braun became the leading figure in the development of space and missile programs, eventually playing a pivotal role in the Apollo moon missions.

- **Arthur Rudolph**: Another key figure from the V-2 rocket program, Rudolph became the project director of the Saturn V rocket program at NASA, the rocket that would eventually bring astronauts to the moon.

- **Hermann Oberth**: Often considered one of the founding fathers of rocketry and astronautics, Oberth was another significant figure brought to the U.S., though his involvement in Nazi activities was less pronounced than some others.

- **Kurt Blome**: A high-ranking Nazi scientist who admitted to conducting deadly experiments on concentration camp prisoners. Despite this, he was acquitted at the Nuremberg Doctors' Trial and then recruited by the U.S. Army Chemical Corps under Operation Paperclip.

- **Hubertus Strughold**: Known as the "father of space medicine," Strughold made significant contributions to aerospace medicine. Controversially, he was also implicated (though not conclusively proven) in some of the medical experiments carried out in Nazi concentration camps.

- **Various Engineers and Scientists**: Beyond these notable figures, Operation Paperclip brought over 1,600 German scientists, engineers, and technicians to the U.S. Many of them held positions of importance in sectors ranging from aeronautics to chemicals to electronics.

EXPOSURE:

The details surrounding Operation Paperclip were not exactly a tightly held secret from the outset. While certain specifics, especially related to the backgrounds of some of the scientists and their Nazi affiliations, were kept hidden or downplayed, the fact that the U.S. was recruiting German scientists after World War II was relatively well-known. However, the full extent and ethical implications became clearer to the public over time.

As early as the 1940s and 1950s, there were media reports highlighting the recruitment of German scientists by the U.S. government. The reports didn't always delve into the ethical issues, but the activity wasn't entirely clandestine.

Over time, more detailed background checks and revelations came to light, particularly concerning the Nazi affiliations of some of the key figures involved. This began to draw more scrutiny and criticism.

By the 1970s, with a growing focus on government accountability and transparency, Congressional inquiries began delving into various covert operations, including Operation Paperclip. The Church Committee, for example, was instrumental in investigating and exposing various intelligence activities.

As the more sordid details emerged, especially regarding the whitewashing of Nazi backgrounds, there was increased public and media criticism of the operation.

Over the decades, historians, journalists, and researchers have worked to uncover more about Operation Paperclip, its participants, and its implications. This has further expanded the public's understanding of its scope and controversies.

Throughout the late 20th century and into the 21st century, various documents related to Operation Paperclip have been declassified, providing a more transparent look at the operation's processes and decisions.

Books like *Operation Paperclip: The Secret Intelligence Program that Brought Nazi Scientists to America* by Annie Jacobsen have extensively researched and detailed the operation, shedding light on its darker aspects and raising awareness among the general public.

In summary, while the existence of Operation Paperclip was not a secret from its inception, the full range of its activities, especially the more controversial aspects, emerged over decades through media reporting, historical research, and declassified documents. Many of the controversial aspects had been suspected but dismissed. Our government knew what it was doing and when asked would deflect or deny the scientists were or had been Nazis.

FALLOUT:

The revelations about Operation Paperclip and the deeper understanding of its scope and implications have had lasting impacts on public perception, governmental accountability, and historical evaluations of the Cold War era. Here are some of the key points of fallout:

- **Ethical Reckoning**: One of the most significant aspects of the fallout was a deeper ethical examination of the decision to bring, and in many cases protect, scientists who had been involved with the Nazi regime. While some of these individuals had been members of the Nazi Party out of societal pressure or career necessity, others were more deeply involved in its war crimes or used slave labor in their projects. The revelations sparked debates on the balance between securing strategic advantages and upholding moral principles.

- **Impact on U.S. Government's Image**: The acknowledgment that the U.S. had actively recruited, protected, and employed former Nazis damaged the U.S. government's image both domestically and internationally, particularly given the nation's stance on the moral high ground after WWII.

- **Influence on U.S. Programs**: The scientists and engineers brought over under Operation Paperclip had significant roles in various U.S. programs, most notably NASA and various defense projects. While their contributions were undeniable (e.g., the Apollo moon landings), there was criticism and unease about the origins of some of this knowledge and expertise.

- **Governmental Accountability**: The uncovering of Operation Paperclip's full scope and the subsequent controversies surrounding it played a role in the push for greater transparency and accountability in U.S. intelligence and defense operations. It fit into a broader narrative during the 1970s, where operations like COINTELPRO, MKULTRA, and others came under scrutiny.

- **Historical Re-evaluation**: Historians and scholars have used Operation Paperclip as a lens to re-evaluate the complexities of the early Cold War era. It's seen as evidence of the pragmatic, and sometimes morally questionable, decisions made in the face of the perceived existential threat from the Soviet Union.

- **Cultural Impact**: Operation Paperclip has been referenced in numerous books, films, and TV shows, often as a point of intrigue, controversy, or conspiracy. Its revelations have fueled distrust in government operations and have been a touchstone for other conspiracy theories.

In the broader view, Operation Paperclip serves as a stark reminder of the moral complexities inherent in global geopolitics, particularly during periods of intense rivalry and perceived existential threats.

Chapter 9
THE US PUBLIC HEALTH SERVICE SYPHILIS STUDY IN GUATEMALA

FROM 1946 TO 1948, the U.S. Public Health Service, in collaboration with the Guatemalan government and the Pan American Sanitary Bureau (a precursor to the Pan American Health Organization), conducted a series of human experiments in Guatemala. These experiments were designed to study the effects and treatment of several sexually transmitted infections, primarily syphilis, but also gonorrhea and chancroid.

ORIGINS:

The U.S. Public Health Service Syphilis Study in Guatemala had its origins in a convergence of medical research interests, the geopolitics of the time, and the readily available vulnerable populations in Guatemala. Let's delve deeper into its origins and the key figures involved:

After World War II, there was heightened interest in understanding and treating sexually transmitted infections (STIs), especially among military personnel. Syphilis was of particular concern because of its widespread prevalence and debilitating effects. The U.S. wanted to test the efficacy of penicillin as a prophylactic against syphilis, and research was directed towards that aim.

The infamous Tuskegee Syphilis Study was already in progress by this time. However, the observational nature of the Tuskegee study (i.e., watching the natural progression of untreated syphilis in already-infected individuals) meant it wasn't suited to testing treatments. A new study was sought, where researchers could deliberately infect subjects and then attempt to cure them.

Guatemala was seen as an advantageous location for such a study due to the existing relationship between the U.S. Public Health Service (USPHS) and the Guatemalan government. There was also a belief (however misguided) that regulations and oversight would be more lenient in Guatemala than in the U.S.

. . .

KEY PLAYERS:

- **Dr. John C. Cutler**: A central figure in the Guatemala experiments, Dr. Cutler was a physician with the USPHS. He was directly involved in executing the experiments on the ground in Guatemala. Notably, after the Guatemala study, Cutler would later go on to have a role in the Tuskegee Syphilis Study.

- **Dr. Thomas Parran Jr.**: As the U.S. Surgeon General at the time, Parran was aware of and implicitly approved the Guatemala experiments. He was a vocal advocate for syphilis research and the need to understand and combat the disease.

- **Guatemalan Government Officials**: The Guatemalan government was complicit in the experiments, with various officials, including those in the military and health departments, allowing the study to proceed. Specific figures in the Guatemalan government were collaborators in the project.

- **Pan American Sanitary Bureau (PASB)**: The PASB, a precursor to the Pan American Health Organization (PAHO), played a role in facilitating the experiments. This was part of a broader collaboration between the U.S. and Latin American health services.

The origin and execution of the Guatemala syphilis experiments are indicative of a period when ethical standards for medical research were either not established or not strictly adhered to, but we believe that hasn't changed.

METHODS AND SUBJECTS:
Methods:
- Intentional Exposure: One of the most egregious aspects of the experiments was the intentional infection of subjects. The researchers used various methods to achieve this:

- **Direct Inoculation**: Researchers introduced the syphilis-causing bacteria directly to the bodies of subjects. This was often done by making small abrasions on the genitals, face, or arms of the participants and then applying syphilis-infected material to the area.
- **Use of Infected Sex Workers**: Some male subjects were exposed to syphilis by contact with infected commercial sex workers. The researchers had purposefully infected these sex workers with syphilis and then facilitated their contact with subjects.
- **Intraspinal Injections**: In some instances, syphilis-causing bacteria were

directly introduced into the spinal fluid of subjects.

- **Monitoring and Treatment**:

Once infected, subjects were observed for signs and symptoms of the disease. Various interventions were tried, including the use of penicillin, to ascertain its efficacy in preventing or treating the infection. However, not all subjects received adequate treatment.

Many of the participants were neither informed about the nature and purpose of the experiments nor were they aware they were being infected with syphilis or other STIs. Moreover, efforts were made to ensure subjects remained in controlled environments, like prisons or asylums, so they could be easily monitored.

Subjects:

The choice of subjects was deeply problematic, targeting the most vulnerable sections of society who had little or no power to object or provide informed consent.

- **Soldiers**: Members of the Guatemalan military were among the primary subjects. The military setting provided a controlled environment for the researchers.

- **Prisoners**: The confined environment of prisons made inmates a convenient target for these experiments. Both male and female prisoners were subjected to the study, with some male prisoners being exposed to syphilis through contact with infected sex workers.
- **Mental Health Patients**: Institutions housing patients with mental health challenges were also locations for these experiments. The inherent vulnerabilities of these patients, combined with the confined nature of asylums, made them prime targets.
- **Commercial Sex Workers**: Sex workers were both subjects and instruments in the experiments. Many were intentionally infected with syphilis to further the research goals.
- **Orphans**: There is evidence to suggest that children in orphanages were also involved, though the exact extent and nature of their involvement remain less clear than with other groups.

In total, it's estimated that up to 1,500 people were

subjected to these experiments. Many never received adequate treatment, and the long-term health consequences for these individuals and their descendants remain largely unquantified.

The methods and choice of subjects used in the Guatemala syphilis study reflect a stark disregard for individual rights, ethics, and basic human decency, making it one of the darkest episodes in the history of medical research.

EXPOSURE:

The U.S. Public Health Service Syphilis Study in Guatemala remained relatively unknown to the public for decades after its conclusion until Dr. Susan Reverby, a Wellesley College historian, came across references to the Guatemala experiment while conducting research on the Tuskegee Syphilis Study. Reverby was sifting through archived papers of Dr. John C. Cutler, one of the primary investigators involved in both the Guatemala and Tuskegee studies.

In her research, Reverby uncovered documents detailing the unethical methods and procedures used in the Guatemala study. Recognizing the significance of her findings, she took it upon herself to delve deeper, resulting in a detailed account of the experiments.

Dr. Reverby initially shared her findings at academic conferences and subsequently published her research. The revelations caused shockwaves in both the medical community and the general public. The immediate reaction was one of horror and disbelief, with many comparing the Guatemala experiments to the Tuskegee Syphilis Study.

Following the exposure, the U.S. government was quick to respond.

In 2010, then U.S. Secretary of State Hillary Clinton and Secretary of Health and Human Services Kathleen Sebelius issued a joint formal apology to the people of Guatemala and to all those affected by the experiments. They condemned the research as unethical and inhumane.

FALLOUT:

In response to the revelations, President Barack Obama ordered the Presidential Commission for the Study of Bioethical Issues to review the Guatemala experiments and ensure that current rules for research participants protect their health and well-being. The Commission's findings reinforced the unethical nature of the study and highlighted areas for improvement in current research ethics.

The Guatemalan government also reacted strongly to the revelations, expressing deep concern and disappointment. The country initiated its own investigation into the experiments to ascertain the full extent of the harm done to its citizens.

As details about the study emerged, it received extensive media coverage, with many outlets highlighting the ethical lapses and comparing the experiments in Guatemala with the infamous Tuskegee study.

The exposure of the Guatemala syphilis experiments serves as a potent reminder of the importance of transparency, oversight, and ethical considerations in medical research. The uncovering of this hidden chapter underscores the value of historical research and the importance of vigilance to ensure such transgressions are not repeated in the future.

But have similar experiments been conducted since? It's a fair question to ask, especially since we're all living in a post-Covid world. We now are confident Covid came from a lab, not from a wet market which we were told was the case. Will we find out decades from now that the entire world were victims to a medical experiment?

Chapter 10
OPERATION LAC (LARGE AREA COVERED)

OPERATION LAC (LARGE AREA COVERAGE) was a secret U.S. Army experiment conducted in the 1950s. The primary aim was to assess the dispersion patterns of chemical substances in the atmosphere.

ORIGINS:

Operation LAC (Large Area Coverage) originated during the Cold War, a period marked by intense rivalry and suspicion between the United States and the Soviet Union. Both superpowers were heavily invested in research and development related to warfare capabilities, which included nuclear, chemical, and biological weapons. Given this backdrop, the U.S. military was keen on understanding the potential threats posed by chemical and biological warfare, as well as developing potential countermeasures.

By the mid-20th century, advancements in technology, especially aviation, meant that large-scale chemical or biological attacks were plausible. Bombers could potentially release these agents over vast swathes of territory, affecting large populations. Hence, it was deemed crucial for the U.S. military to understand how these agents would disperse and travel if they were released.

Understanding the dispersal patterns of chemical or biological agents would serve a dual purpose. On the one hand, it would aid in developing defense mechanisms and responses against potential enemy attacks. On the other, it would provide the U.S. with data for its own offensive capabilities should it choose to deploy such weapons.

Given the scope and significance of the operation — spreading materials over vast portions of U.S. territory — it's plausible that Eisenhower and other high-ranking officials in his administration were aware of it, especially since national defense and preparedness were high priorities during the Cold War era.

However, it's important to note that not every detail of every operation would necessarily be presented directly to the president, especially in the intricate bureaucracy of defense and intelligence operations. The president would be briefed on many defense and intelligence matters, but whether he knew the specific details or just the broader goals and findings is not always clear from public records.

As with many covert operations of the era, direct evidence of presidential knowledge might be found in declassified documents or archives, if at all. Some operations remain classified or partially obscured to this day. It's also possible that the details of such operations were known to only a select few within the administration, with others being aware only of the general goals and findings.

IMPLEMENTATION:

In the late 1950s, the U.S. Army Chemical Corps initiated Operation LAC to study large-scale chemical dispersal patterns. The operation would involve the release of a chemical tracer over vast portions of the U.S. territory.

The compound selected for the tests was zinc cadmium sulfide, a fluorescent powder. It was chosen because it could be easily detected, even in minute quantities, allowing for effective tracking of dispersal patterns. At the time of the tests, it was considered to be a harmless substance.

The U.S. Army used aircraft to disseminate the zinc cadmium sulfide, releasing it over various parts of the United States. The scale of the operation was significant, with many tests conducted across multiple states.

HEALTH RISKS:

Operation LAC (Large Area Coverage) involved the dispersal of zinc cadmium sulfide, a fluorescent powder, over various parts of the U.S. to study wind currents and particle dispersion patterns. At the time of the tests, it was believed that zinc cadmium sulfide was a relatively harmless substance, which is why it was chosen as a tracer material.

However, later studies and concerns raised questions about the health implications of cadmium compounds. Cadmium is a heavy metal that, when ingested or inhaled in sufficient amounts, can have toxic effects on the kidneys and bones and may also increase the risk of cancer. Chronic exposure to cadmium can result in a range of health problems.

While large areas were covered during Operation LAC, the actual amount of zinc cadmium sulfide that an individual might have inhaled would likely be small.

However, the full extent of the exposure and its cumulative effects, especially given repeated tests, is unclear.

The U.S. National Research Council conducted a review in the 1990s about the potential health risks of the Army's zinc cadmium sulfide dispersion program, including Operation LAC. The review concluded that the exposures were likely low and did not pose a risk to human health. However, some have critiqued this conclusion, arguing that not enough is known about the health effects of chronic low-level exposure to cadmium compounds.

EXPOSURE:

The exposure of Operation LAC (Large Area Coverage) and similar tests came to wider public knowledge years after the tests were conducted. Here's how it was exposed:

- **Declassified Information**: The U.S. Department of Defense and the U.S. Army released information about these tests in the 1970s and 1990s. The official disclosures shed light on the extent and nature of the tests.

- **Public Research and Media Reports**: The revelations about Operation LAC and similar tests were picked up by researchers, journalists, and activists.

Media reports on the tests brought the information to a wider audience, sparking public debate and concern.

- **Congressional Inquiries**: As with many controversial operations that were later revealed, there were calls for transparency and investigations at various governmental levels, including by members of Congress. These inquiries led to further disclosure of details and, in some cases, official apologies or statements of regret.

- **Subsequent Investigations**: After the initial revelations, there were calls for further investigation into the potential health impacts of the tests. As mentioned earlier, organizations like the U.S. National Research Council undertook reviews in the 1990s to ascertain the health risks of the zinc cadmium sulfide dispersion tests.

The exposure of Operation LAC and other similar tests led to significant public concern, not only about the potential health impacts but also about the ethics of conducting such tests on an unknowing public. These revelations prompted discussions about government transparency, the rights of citizens, and the balance between national security interests and public health and safety.

. . .

FALLOUT (NO PUN INTENDED):

Given the later understanding of cadmium's potential health risks, there have been concerns and criticisms from the public and researchers about the ethics and safety of Operation LAC and similar tests.

While the consensus from official reviews is that the health risks from Operation LAC were minimal, the very fact that such tests were conducted on an unknowing public has caused understandable concern and criticism. The potential long-term health impacts on specific individuals, particularly those who might have had heightened susceptibility or pre-existing health conditions, are difficult to ascertain fully.

IS OPERATION LAC STILL ONGOING?

Many will cite the conspiracy theory of chemtrails as a fact that Operation LAC is still ongoing in some capacity. However, when anyone in authority is asked, they dismiss the theory of chemtrails as simply a tinfoil hat conspiracy theory. Given the government has played with dispersing chemicals in the air before, why would they stop or not do it again.

CONCLUSION

Within the pages of *Conspiracy Theories That Were True*, we delved deep into stories once cast aside, seen as mere tales for late-night radio shows or the fodder of wild imaginations. The revelations of Operation LAC, Operation Mockingbird, MKULTRA, and others, however, have realigned our understanding, cautioning us against the swift dismissal of ideas, however outlandish they may initially seem.

In today's lexicon, the phrase "conspiracy theory" too often evokes a smirk or a knowing glance. It's become synonymous with the fringe, the unfounded, the sensationalist. Yet, as the chapters of this book illustrate, yesterday's ridicule can transform into today's documented fact. Time and again, whispers once rele-

About the Author

Ethan Hayes grew up in Oklahoma and moved to Texas when he attended Texas A&M. Upon graduation he was hired by Texas Parks and Wildlife and remained there until he retired twenty-two years later. He currently lives in southeast Texas with his wife and two dogs. When he's not spending time enjoying the outdoors and writing, he sips a cold beer on his front porch while listening to Bluegrass music.

Send in your encounter story:
encountersbigfoot@gmail.com

Also by Ethan Hayes

ENCOUNTERS IN THE WOODS

WHAT LURKS BEYOND

FEAR IN THE FOREST

INTO THE DARKNESS

ENCOUNTERS BIGFOOT

TALES OF TERROR

I SAW BIGFOOT

STALKED: TERRIFYING TRUE CRIME STORIES

CONSPIRACY THEORIES THAT WERE TRUE

Also by Free Reign Publishing

STAT: CRAZY MEDICAL STORIES

MYSTERIES IN THE DARK

13 PAST MIDNIGHT

THINGS IN THE WOODS

LOVE ENCOUNTERS

gated to the peripheries of societal belief have come to stand as undeniable historical truths.

That's not to say we should take all theories at face value. A discerning mind must sift through layers of misinformation, bias, and sometimes sheer fantasy. But history beckons us with a clear message: Keep an open mind. The truth isn't always what it first appears to be, and sometimes the most vehement denials mask the deepest secrets.

How many of today's scoffed-at speculations will be the verified truths of tomorrow? In our age of information ubiquity, where digital footprints are almost impossible to erase entirely and global connectivity brings collective scrutiny to even the most hidden corners, it is likely that more suppressed truths will emerge from the fog of doubt.

To the seekers of truth, this book serves as both a compass and a challenge. A compass, directing us to always seek out deeper understanding and knowledge, even in the face of skepticism or mockery. And a challenge, urging us to be the vanguards of inquiry, pushing boundaries and questioning accepted narratives.

In closing, as we stand on the precipice of an era where information is both our greatest asset and our most profound challenge, let's remember the lessons from these once-dismissed tales. Let us never stop prob-

CONCLUSION

ing, questioning, and unearthing. For truth, no matter how deeply buried or obscured, will always find its way to light, urging us to listen, learn, and most importantly, to evolve.

— Ethan Hayes

CONTINUE WITH OTHER GREAT BOOKS BY BESTSELLING AUTHOR, ETHAN HAYES
or
READ OTHER GREAT TITLES BY
FREE REIGN PUBLISHING

STAT: CRAZY MEDICAL STORIES

www.ingramcontent.com/pod-product-compliance
Lightning Source LLC
Chambersburg PA
CBHW030621070426
42449CB00041B/961